BECOMING UNTIL
poems

Marjorie J. Levine

the three
tomatoes
The Three Tomatoes Book Publishing

Published January 2024

ISBN: 979-8-9891962-5-8
Library of Congress Control Number: 2024900934

For information address:
The Three Tomatoes Book Publishing
6 Soundview Rd.
Glen Cove, NY 11542
www.thethreetomatoespublishing.com

Cover and interior design: Susan Herbst

Cover and author photo: Frederick Piccarello

Last page photo: Marjorie J. Levine

for the girl looking out of the back bedroom window at 779

CONTENTS

HAIKUS

STREET POEMS

MAGICAL THINKING

HAIKUS

A SIDE GLANCE

Yesterday is still

Inside me like a new view

I hold on tightly.

EVERYTHNG ENDS

After the good deeds

The blue sky blended with clouds

Ennui filled the cup.

FADING SLOWLY

Afternoon is gone

The tree bends to the pale light

Footprints fade to dark.

GOING AWAY

Sundown by the bay

The letter now floats away

She walks to the night.

IN THE NIGHT SKY
ABOVE THE CITY AVENUE

The moon high above

One star below on the left

Both move and shine bright.

MANHATTAN

Driving south one day

Miles spill over shoulders

I was almost home.

MEDITATION MYSTERY

Alone in body

Who am I to determine

The sweet soul of self.

NORTH

Red house in grey sky

Who sleeps next to those branches

In the dim soft light.

ONE DIRECTION

Signs point to one way

And it was the only place

To find memories.

SERIOUSLY

In all seasons here

Time bends to the azure sea

But leaves me paler.

SHARP TONES

As the grey comes in

Shades turn to crisp clarity

And shine old to new.

THE BEND IN THE VIEW

She who once lived there

So long ago would shed tears

To see this new view.

THE BLACK VELVET DRESS

The black velvet dress

So long ago I lost it

Never since replaced.

THERE'S SOMETHING ABOUT THE NIGHT

The darkness at night

The grey soul spirit above

The past in green light.

THIS VIEW FOR WHOSE EYES

This unbroken view

Caught my eye in October

One light day at dusk.

THROUGH A PARTICULAR
KALEIDOSCOPE LENS

Time passed in this house

Where I had magical dreams

And now I am old.

TOGETHER

The beach at sunrise

The sand under soft blue mist

Two hands bind morning.

TOPEKA CAN BE
WHATEVER YOU WANT IT TO BE

Topeka in sun

Will soon change to Topeka

In white crystal snow.

VIEWS IN AFTERTHOUGHTS

This was the first spot

Where I saw the pale stranger

Then he went away.

WAXING CRESCENT

Illuminated

In a shiny blue night sky

Twigs tremble and freeze.

WHAT'S LEFT

Light blue to dark blue

The curtain fell on water

Rocks remained so strong.

WINDOWS

Through a lens long gone

There was magic in the view

Past is so quisquous.

WISCONSIN DELLS

The huge movie screen

Sits behind the red flowers

In Wisconsin Dells.

A DEATH IN THE VALLEY

One life dead ended

The day he left the blue stream

And rode to the hills.

FORTUITOUS HIGHWAY

His right was her left

So they met in the middle

Love bended two hearts.

SOMBER

She moves as one young

And one day she will be old

A different face.

THE OLD STREET

Going back that day

Was a huge mistake to make

The street had cobwebs.

THE VIOLET TULIP

Is the color right

Is the flower really pink

Eyes closed last summer.

TONE DEAF

The widow sat still

Hearing wind on Saturday

A new man brought songs.

TRACES OF SAND ON A CITY STREET

After a hot day

The green beach towel was lost

On concrete tan stones.

LIGHTHOUSES

Mist sets on azure

One light beckons through the fog

And brings lost ones home.

LIGHTHOUSES II

Whether under grey

Or under blue, the soft hues

Bring travelers home.

STREET POEMS

BY THE SEA

On Coast Road,
In Larne, two people stand
Between the purple rocky cliffs and the
Pale colorless sea on the other side of
Yellow and purple flowers.

Cars pass by with drivers and passengers
Whose faces I will never see.
There is an open gate with a path that
Leads to an unseen place.

And soon, there is a sign that says,
"Boats," and then the sky turns magically blue.
But, in the distance the clouds are so low that
They touch the water.

DELICATE BRUSHSTROKES

In Eck en Wiel,
At the end of the street
There is a signpost with four different
Directions to point the way to quiet
Houses still standing alongside beautiful
Canals that take wanderers to places with
Other beautiful canals.

Go to the little graveyard, where people
Rest under the blue and green.
A place this beautiful might perhaps
Exist only in the imagination, in places
Where the weary and forlorn might go to find
Peace when breathless dreams fall away.

Keep going to arrive at a place to rest
And a place to go once around, go
Around and around and around and never
Leave because all here want to stay longer
Because this is a place so beautiful, so
Perfectly decorated with delicate and perfect
Brushstrokes, that nobody ever leaves.

EASY STREET

On Roxbury Drive,
In Beverly Hills, there's an air of
Leafy radiance that settles in and
Lingers until the bewitching hour
When the dusk comes and trances
These special swells into some
Hypnotic splendor.

The dark arrives as usual
And everybody settles in as usual
And there is nothing unusual
In these perfumed rooms.

And then the morning arrives,
The sun rises on this street
Shining a sharp light letting
All those who live on other streets
Know they don't live on easy street.

GOING THE OTHER WAY

On Larimer Street,
In Denver, I went the wrong way
Because the sun was endlessly bright
And my eyes hurt.

So, I winced and decided to turn
Around and see a different view
And go the other way.
I longed for night, so the darkness
Might blur the vision.

In sunlight, there were too many new
Things and I longed for the
Old buildings; these pieces didn't fit.

This music is too now,
And the haircuts are too today.
These silvery parked bicycles
Have taken short trips.
The billiard club fills me with despair
For times gone by so I go over
And look at all the hanging beads for
Making necklaces, as if they held a key to
Some magical thinking and wearing beads
Could bring back what once was.

I wondered if this pawn shop
Accepts memories,
And keeps them safe
Until later when the memories
Are bought back.

Nobody finds places long gone.
But, taking back memories
Makes me smile.
On this street,
It would be fitting.

HOT WATERCOLORS

At Plaja Jupiter,
On Strada Brindisi, look at the
Wonderful things and colorful things:

Rich green and pink stuff to take home
And even more stuff to chew and eat
So the sense of wonder is remembered.

Blue water on one side of the sandy heat
And huge proud swans wait on the water
On the other side, and never move.

Later, the day perhaps will become
Fragmented but the sense of wonder
Might never become blurred.

HOUSES AND HOMES

In Prague,
There is a store with a wonderful wall
Decorated with a picture of a tree at the end of a road.
And sitting under the tree are pictures of
Dogs, birds, and a tiger:
Pictures to show the way when yellow sunlight hits
The wall and the glareless lines are not blurred.

Across from that store is a vacant lot, filled with
Colorful piles of stuff, there from perhaps forever.

I traveled down that road past a bright yellow house
With flower pots on ledges outside the
Bottom floor windows,
There to show a different way: the way home.

I traveled down that road past a short brown house
With only one floor and pale shutters and
Yellow flowers in the garden to show the way
To a different home: this home.

And I traveled down the road past an orange house
With a tree near the gate to obscure the view of: this house.

All houses and homes are on the same street and
All stand so quietly and still and share
The same sense of repose in different
Houses and homes.

If a visitor were to sigh while passing through this street
The sound would shatter this street's tranquility:
Fracture the sense of beauty that lives on this street.

NARROW STREET

In Scanno,
A low and narrow street
Has a quiet outdoor cafe with tables
Covered in yellow tablecloths.

One man dines alone
Next to and under purple
Red and pink flowers.
Gorgeous proud balconies are
Set into buildings with old grey
Chipped and broken stone.

A little store down the path displays
Colorful children's clocks:
Bunnies and elephants and angels
Designed to make the children laugh.

From another high window, freshly washed
Towels hang and down below mothers
Gather to talk and soon walk with their babies.

Flower pots sit on small steps,
Leading up to a home where another woman
Is standing above the street looking down
From a wide open window near a bird feed
And she too is hanging the wash out to dry.

And then nothing moves and all is frozen.
Only the wash; the wash flying in front of that
Large foreboding mountain under a crisp
And clear blue and white sky.

OLD AND NOW

In Lucerne,
There are old and newer
Things and all sort of things to remind
You of recent things.

A blue trolley, a grand stone hotel, a
Yellow casino across from a grey church
Where young men parked bicycles to go
To pray in the picture postcard.

There's a palace, and who lives there?
Then brand new buildings that are tiered
Like wedding cakes brimming with green
Shrubbery and a short little building with
Posters of Superman.

The bike rider passes the orange truck
And then the park, always a park so the living
Can remember these streets, these days,
And then keep going and move on.

ORDINARY THINGS

On Main Street,
In Northport, there is a
Guy standing in the middle of the street
Wearing an orange helmet
And a lady, riding a bicycle on the sidewalk,
Wearing a pale straw sun hat
And two children walking home from school
Wearing book bags and carrying skateboards.

A beautiful house proudly displays the flag,
There are two churches on both sides
When you reach Church Street
And one has lovely pink flowers in front.
There's a post office, a bank,
The fire department announcing
The "Firemen's Fair"...

In front of pristine houses on a crisp clear
Day ordinary things are happening
Where extraordinary things happened.
Nothing remarkable here at all
To speak of the remarkable man that
Once lived here.

Pass through this town, keep driving
Keep going, don't look over your shoulder
Keep going until you reach the end:
The water with the boats and the looming
Hill on the other side
And you know you can't turn back.

PRETTY WALK

On East Guenther Street,
In San Antonio, I felt I should
Be wearing fancy ribbons in my hair
Because the houses are so pretty.

I passed by houses that are
Treasures with artistically sculptured
Facades and stunning lace screened
Verandas where guests might dine
On tea cakes spread out on crisp white
Doilies and later when the sun goes
Down, talk of small things that matter
And rinse their hands in dainty
Finger bowls to keep things fresh.

There's a place to stand to view the
Spot where the breathless
Flowing river passes through
Bringing a sense of sameness.

I got lost on this intoxicating street,
Longed to stay, and knew I could return.
There's a sense of serenity in this old
Comfort as the sunlight falls on this same
Street as it has fallen on this street forever.

REMEMBERING AN OLD STREET

On Main Street,
On Martha's Vineyard, I am
Filled with bittersweet memories.
I remember Main Street...
I was there, so long ago.

I can still smell that ocean air,
So briny and salty and
All those summers come
Flooding back.

The day we ate in the diner
And how the jukebox blared all
The songs we loved.

In spite of all the quaintness
Of that lovely and charming place
I longed with desperation
To be some place else.

I suppose we are what we carry
Inside us and in spite of that
Heady beauty, whenever I was there
I longed to be somewhere else.

I suppose there are places that always
Make us want to go home.

SCENES FROM LONG AGO

On Beard Street,
In Kernersville, there are colorful
Wall murals which give glimpses
Into what was, long ago.

I saw ladies in billowing long
Red and white dresses standing
With gentlemen wearing tall hats
All waiting at the railroad station
For family arriving from faraway places.
Soon, they would all step into a horse
Drawn carriage to take a short ride home.

Nobody looked up to see the child
Perched high above who on bleak days
After school would climb to the flat roof
To wait for the trains to pass.

The trains were carrying weary passengers
Traveling to faraway places, and they were
Also going home.

Many years later, she would remember
The sound of the whistle as the trains
Passed and she would speak of the sound
As both sad and mournful,
Perhaps because it always
Strangely reminded
Her of all times past.

SEEING ALMOST NOTHING

On Repatriation Road,
In Pickering Brook, I drove
For a long time
And saw almost nothing
Except the narrow road
Ahead and trees on both sides
With nothing behind me
And nothing ahead of me.
Then, I saw a tractor on one side
And a low gate on the other and
I knew I was reaching a place.
Some place.

Then, I saw a tiny little house
All alone there behind some flowers.
It had a front porch with old chairs
And some other muted things.
In front of the house was a tree,
Three times taller than the house!
I kept going.
I kept going
Chasing the end of that road.
Until I reached the end of the road.
Literally.
And then I went back home.

SET IN STONE

On Pineview Street,
In Rocky Mount, there is an old cemetery:
The place where the dead go.
One grave had nice fresh pink flowers
To whisper that somebody is missed.

Not many graves, but very old stones
Broken and chipped stones set in tired dirt
Seen through windows of houses that
Line that still street.

Some houses set way back
As if to separate the living
From the dead.

And then, I saw a children's swing set,
And the sun trying to peek through
To perhaps lift a sense of deep gloom.

STANDING STILL

On Højdevangs Allé,
In Copenhagen, the flowers
That line the street
Are so fragrant that two
Women stopped walking.

They stood between two buildings
To look at small blue flowers on
One side while purple and white
Flowers flourished without moving
Behind them, on the other side.

THE LIGHTHOUSE

On Main Street,
In Chatham, there's a lighthouse
Between the red, white, and blue flag
And a white house with a red roof
All at the end of the street.

There are cars looking to park and
Men pushing baby carriages
And women with shopping bags
And everybody is going one way:
To the ocean, to the blue ocean.

There's a lantern there to light
The way back at night to other
Places: to other places near to here
So that the walkers can go
Back the other way to reach home.
And the way is lighted so the drivers
Who have come from far away from here
Never quite reach the end of the street
At the end of the day.

THE LITTLE FLOWER SHOP

In Munich,
There is a charming little
Flower shop in a tiny little building
With a green and white
Striped awning.

It was tempting to stand and
Gaze at the technicolor flattered
Flowers.

But, I spun around to also see
Red flowers on tall stems
In front of a house covered in
Gorgeous green ivy.

THE SWANKY PLACE

On Cherry Street,
In Denver, I suppose nothing
Much has changed.

Maybe some things.
There's a liquor store on one corner
And a Mexican restaurant on the other.
With one breath,
The street is inside of me.

The beckoning street that held
The door through which he left to
Go up to the mountains, see an
Opera, and eat swell food:
The swanky place.

There is comfort in knowing
That not much changes:
In some places, time may indeed
Stand still.

The street is quiet now;
I think nobody is home.
And it does look like it will soon rain.

THESE DAYS

On the Promenade,
In Blackpool, exquisite wonder
And bright colors create an intense
Kaleidoscope of magical fun.

There's a high tower and
Amusements and prizes and
Horse drawn carriages riding next to
Modern cars.

On the pier, there's a Ferris Wheel with
Rotating gondolas perfectly suited for
Grand and glorious views
Of luminous illuminations.

Luminous illuminations
All right by the sea
By the sea, so all the children
Who come here
Will remember these days.

THIS HEADY ELIXIR

On Clifton Hill,
In Niagara Falls, there is a soft intoxicating
Smell in the air of sweet and heady nostalgia.
Walkers cross the street to a bright lush green
Park and the water is then behind them as a
Light mist sprays their backs and the
Visuals turn into blurred memories
Set in stone.

All the excitement is about to begin.
There is a turquoise haunted house,
A beckoning movie theater,
The wax museum,
And a souvenir shop:
It's a massive swirling kaleidoscope of
Dreamlike and almost surreal color.

Then, in the center of all this heady elixir
Is a glorious and perfect SkyWheel,
Where I imagine children sit with parents
High up above it all, setting the graphics into
What will years later seem almost
Hallucinogenic.

MAGICAL THINKING

AT THE END OF THE TUNNEL

She sits wishing something fortuitous will enter her day
And as she types in bold font she finds nothing new to say.
Her work is bland and dull and never cuts with a sharp knife
So she plays chess online to try to mitigate her strife.

Every day is a rerun, nothing different and
Nothing new is ever said
And after watching Buzzr and laughing at Password Plus
She goes to bed.
In her dreams she meets Frankie Avalon
Who asks her out on a date
And when she awakens she truly believes
He could have been her fate.

If truth be told she believes she is delusional
But tries not to pout and mope
Because honestly without her imagination
Each day would be a difficult cope.
Go get this, go get that, go for a drive and go get the mail
A travel brochure arrived and the picture of the
Mediterranean entices her to sail.

So she packs up her stuff and considers taking
A pink cute little bikini
But the last time she wore it she was
Insulted by a crude meanie.
Life is fraught with ups and downs and
Taking chances is hard I know
But at least today she has a future and
She is not yet six feet below.

What is this puzzle on this planet all about

She wonders aloud.
Is there nothing she can leave behind
Of which she can be proud?
She finds a little old black and white photo when
She was little and small
It seems like just yesterday when she wore a diaper
And that was all.

So now she is old and why did the years pass
So quickly into a puddle?
It is bewildering and confusing and a riddle
That seems like a muddle.
She can stick big words and metaphors into this thing
She sits writing
But honestly, at the end of the day would a reader
Find it more biting?

And so another day ends and she pulls up her
Orange weighted blanket.
A new trip will begin and magical thinking
Will be her impetus to crank it.
Then she will return home to a dusty apartment
That needs painting
And for some laughs she will dance the tango
In her lobby and then feign fainting.

That's it! It's all about the comedy and jokes.
Without laughter we simply have no hopes.

BECOMING UNTIL

She knew she was finished and all doors were
Closed, a chapter had ended and though sad, she felt
Vaguely imposed.

She thought she loved him as he seduced her with flattery,
But as the time passed, she felt like a victim of
Mental battery.

Her love was like a mirage, a thought trapped inside her head
It was a delusion around rumination when at night
She went to bed.
It is hard to not hold on, to let go of what sustained her
On cold nights...
And what was harder still was to find a new path with
Different delights.

Some live on the surface, never having heartache
Over trivial things
While others live within deep desire always
Wanting to catch brass rings.

She wears herself out with her silly passions and such
The truth is she must have not mattered much.
Now she watches from her window as the trains pass
And hope drizzles in all lit
She waits and waits for just one to step off and somehow be
A magical perfect fit.

She bends and at the end of the day, after all is said
And the air is still
She sits on her green porch and she changes her thoughts...
And becomes "until."

BLUE SKY WHITE SNOW

White driven soft snow with no direction had fallen
On a cold settled January bitter remorseless day...
And I left a familiar road to go crawlin'
Along this path with bare trees that was called
Destination Way.

Under soft clouds and a crisp defined blue high sky
I left small footprints and then saw a face in
A window reminding me it was a time long ago
That I had said good- bye
To that old streetlight which was still there to
Curate a change to sow.

CONTEMPLATION

Within all the sights
All I could see was sadness
Alone in the still.

An old bus in the view
Yesterday going to there
Today is nowhere.

The acquired taste is perceiving
Time in a blue sky hanging over
The old gas station.

DON'T USE THAT WORD ON TUESDAYS

I went downstairs to the quiet main lobby at about noon
And much to my chagrin the mail was not in,
It was too soon!

I grumbled and complained and let it be known
That receiving the mail is a major activity for this old crone.

I shouted: "Darn, I came down here for nothing
And I am mad!"
I continued to rant: "The mail delivered late is just so bad."

A neighbor walked in and took a bite of a donut on the table
Then another man in a uniform came in to repair the cable.

The dentist went out to go around the corner for a bite
The massage therapist helped a mommy feel alright.

And little Jackie went to the park to go fly his kite.
And during this fiasco, the carpenter did not take flight.

I pondered if I should vent and cut loose.
Finally, a dancer turned to me and said
In a most cryptic way:

"Don't use that word on Tuesdays."
Now this is a true tale I kid you not
I appreciate her bon mots a lot.

GREEN STREETS

I always knew serenity was
Measured by the shades of green
On roads at almost blue dawn in summer.

I searched for the perfect quiet town
With stone paths that were muted in soft
Watercolors at dusk and when the
Streetlights were lit they always
Showed the way home.

The perfect spot became cool in fall
And was washed in white when winter
Months arrived to let those on the street
Know that special days would soon be celebrated.

There had to be a main street with small stores
And a quaint movie theater that showed films
That children would later remember as adults.

And the insides of the homes were quiet and peaceful
And filled with what was right for everybody.
So… I found that place.

There are railroad tracks to take you away
And the same tracks are there to bring you back...
But nobody goes anywhere.

And those passing by can almost smell
Paradise: a heady mix of
Romance with magic in the air.

IN THE GLOAMING

My friend John went to Belize and found
Seduction by the sea
And when he told me about his place
I knew that it was not for me.

Joan traveled to Corviglia mountain to ski
And had a great week
But her lofty and majestic adventure I knew
I would not seek.

Diane lay on the white sandy beach of Estoril
And basked in the sun,
Quite frankly and honestly her vacation was not
My idea of fun.

For what do I yearn and what do I seek?
I will give you all a slight brief peek.

I would love to reside on a particular
Green street so in the morning I can hear
The hearts of the doves beat.

And in the orange fall when the sun goes down
And all is dark, I can maybe go for a quiet walk
Or bike ride in a park.

I do not need anything fancy or remarkable to be
So nice, but a warm house on a corner with a
Streetlight seems like paradise.

LIMERENCE

Why am I feeling all this great emotion?
Perhaps I am thinking of poor Mary,
Moving away after so long living
In a quietly familiar and convenient place.
Mary, audibly rocking and rocking in the
Same chair above me as she aged into invisibility…
And soon I too will leave this same place.
For how long did I live with illusions,
Locking away all transitory possibilities
And realities and choosing instead to
Dwell inside mercurial fantasies and
Interior delusions and then grounding a still life?
Now the fading obstacles hardly matter.
The grey heavy details carved and set in stones
Have been kicked away by newer shades
Of sharp pastels that do not even belong
To me in my particular smallness.
Fog is moving in from the Hudson River,
Passing over yesterday and all the
Layered stories and everything
That came… before.

LOSS

There came an unexpected loss which melted into blue regret
After the last smooth wave of orange autumn settled into
The anticipation of a great white blinding snowfall
At a time when everything was strangely
Falling away.

After thoughts of what might have been and blurry pages
Were turned, this death carved deep melancholy into my
New grey days and I walked a little slower under
Cloudy skies and icy streets and tried to see new possibilities
Through a hazy window that has been my unchanging view
Since forever.

LUCID DREAMING

Inspiration comes from unexpected places
Especially from others with smiling expressions
On their faces.
So I took pen in hand for a lofty literary review
And at midnight, after eating a late snack,
I had something to do.

My previous work was labeled filled with "self-pity!"
I internalized that opinion and decided to be more witty.
But I pondered that conclusion and it seemed
A puzzling disconnect.
It was a bewildering deduction; .
I did a quick mental 360: should I be wrecked?

I began to think: was I being "extra" as I crafted sad poems
Or was I just branding my special form of high end
Well praised tomes?
How can some be critical about pieces
Filled with melancholy
And think that other work would be greater
If they were jolly?
But, I investigated what is "trending" and
Causing much chatter and I decided to get
Laser focused on a difficult matter.
I was told "sex sells" and of course that is not surprising
But, with my new interests I prefer word designing.

I decided to be more cheerful and cut back on the sorrow
I analyzed my mantra and I look forward to tomorrow.
I put on my Gucci tee and my bag labeled Christian Dior
And lo and behold my neighbors embraced me for
Never being a bore.

They greeted me in the lobby with high fives
And welcomes and such
And we went to a party and devoured
Chocolate ice cream much.
Will this poem go viral and get the attention of Kanye?
I contacted him on twitter and asked
"Whatta ya know, whatta ya say?"
He did not answer but I imagined that Sharon Olds
And Louise Gluck chuckled in replies and asked me
To join them for tea at a place with clout.

We time traveled to the famous and legendary
Algonquin Round Table and I asked
For a cola and a pumpernickel bagel.

OMG a few tables away sat the infamous and
Brilliant Michio Kaku...
He was gobsmacked that we went through a wormhole
And said: "Who knew?"
Whatever... let's go back to 2023 with haste
We have much to do.
I hope this poem I do not have to edit
If I do, I want engraved in
The Library of Congress that credit.

.

OCEAN PARKWAY

This is the place:
Where time seems to stand still
And only the clouds move above
To show those under the mercurial sky
That the weather is changing.

Decades ago:
I looked down from a window
In a building high over Ocean Parkway.
I can still taste my aunt's sweet turkey dinner
On the day the red ripe cranberries rolled
Over my pink tongue.

That day:
On a bench,
The reader in a blue suit read his book
As a girl sat in a blue dress on another bench
And watched a rider pass on a blue bike
Going to a grey building down a shady road.

Now:
So many years later another face
Looks out of that same window and watches
An old man on a bench read a grey newspaper
As an old lady throws crumbs to feed pigeons.

In the rain:
A car passes going south and then
Slows down to a red light, a red light that
Only stops movement for a minute
A minute of time on Ocean Parkway.

ONE THING IS CERTAIN

It's hard to end any journey
Especially after so much has
Been left unsaid,
Unsaid like a guest who stays
For rainy days and summer nights
And forgets the particulars
Of all the small yesterdays.

So many empty spaces remain
So many holes are ripped within the
Pieces and answers just fall away
Like orange leaves in autumn under a
Dim night street lamp.

Of this she is certain: men
Shared her bed for decades…
They of many different mercurial
Faces and she was loved,
Defined in bittersweet murky ways
Within truths she concealed
In her own particular brand of
Hidden unfolding dark celluloid.

In almost old age, she peels off her layers
And sheds her lizard skin
And lets who she was supposed to be
Be, and then lets a facade fall away…
To deserted playgrounds, and moldy theaters,
And haunted highways.

Eventually it will hardly matter when today's
Grandchildren give birth to new babies.

PARADISE IN SHADES OF
GREEN AND ORANGE

I awakened with a start and wanted to see paradise:
I thought eyeballing a different view would be nice.

I knew where to go, I knew what I wanted to see
These days it does not take much to create a happy me.

So I gazed at a town that resembled Willoughby to me
And as I looked and looked I saw what I needed to see.

I saw a brick road covered in orange leaves
After months of green… and when I saw a
Magical streetlight I knew this was my scene!

I packed my bags and waved bye to neighbors and
Locked up my place and soon I settled in to a quiet
New town that I called my space.

Now this poem should not be considered sad...
So do not be mad.

I wanted to create a happy poem for
My readers and friends… after all,
Everything I do has to have laughing ends.

REALITY CHECK

I went to the doctor today
And she did not have much to say.

She diagnosed me with limerence
And suggested help.
"What? And cure myself of magical thinking
And end with a welp?"

SLIPPING AWAY

After passing a high crooked junk pile
And moving further down the road
There is a small wooden house with
A porch with three empty seats
And a blue bicycle with no wheels.
In an open broken box, mail sits
Waiting to be opened and read.

Across the street there is another house
With a large green lawn and a swing set
And two small dogs run around
While a lion sits locked in a cage.

There is another tiny old house
With one grey chair on a bent patio
And a Christmas wreath on the door
Although it is sunny in June.

Then there is a house with red roses
And white tulips that hang high
Over the top of dusty windows.

All of this slips away and falls away
And eventually can be seen only
In rear view mirrors.

But then there is an old church
And this must be the place where
All those who live on this road
Go to pray.

STORM

Wednesday:
It was a perfect storm
On a particular almost desolate highway.
The curves in the grounded road were often
Filled with traffic but on stormy days,
Sometimes not.

There was a sudden presence on one day
One hard rainy day when water filled the air
In moments that gathered and pushed to
A new present with water and visible
Angled lightning that passed in the rear view.

One life, that on most stripped down days
Barely mattered to many or oddly even any,
Turned and that dusk was carved into memory.

On that day, it was a blurry remarkable
Occurrence that happened in almost
Darkness, when the grey ripples
Of thunder in the air parted and
Forced her to listen to nothing.
But she remembered,
She remembered… to slow down.

And then with no warning,
A rapid appearance startled.
And right, moving to left,
From one side to the other side
Two old bent strangers with
No umbrellas, but holding hands…
Crossed the road.

THE TREE

Decades ago, I had a little tree in my backyard
And waiting so long for it to grow was very hard.
I waited many years for that tree to grow so tall
And complete... and I loved how it appeared in
The summer concrete heat.

When I looked out of my window, all I saw
Were washes of solid green...
Only a few others could even understand
What that image could mean.

Much to my dismay, one day I heard a racket
And that tree was cut down
And nothing was the same
With the image of the green gone
From my side of town.

THE YELLOW HORIZON

In summer, or fall, winter, or spring
That dusty road delivered no brass ring.

Nothing ever changed and in the twilight
There was no difference between day or night.

The green faded to a sunset so yellow
When winter came, the whites were mellow.

Spring beckoned: a path different, eternal, muted and refined.
She was lifted from the sedentary because a stranger
Passed so kind.

TWO VIEWS

The strong wind knocked something
Over and when I looked through the
Window and saw under a streetlight
The way he was looking at her,
I realized life had passed me by.

The strong wind knocked something
Over and when she looked through the
Window and saw under a streetlight
The way he was looking at her,
She realized life had passed her by.

VIEWS IN AFTERTHOUGHTS II

In the light right here
I returned to the same place
Where I first met him.

The water under
The distant high silver bridge
Spoke of profound loss.

THE BEND IN THE HIGHWAY

On this morning, she gazes into the mirror
And sees a stranger...
Within everything that came before,
This image should speak of danger.

The idea of walking within this new picture
Speaks of alarm
But she embraces the view with no hint
Of any disarm.

In the light of this new sunrise, with time
Chasing her to passage
She decides to not carry around what
Could be considered baggage.

And after so long a time, there surfaced
Something new... something sweet,
So although the exterior is a perspective that
Could spell defeat…

She sees the fresh watercolors in her painting
And feels the wind so strong
She moves forward and turns a corner
And puts on new shoes and hurries along.

ACKNOWLEDGMENTS

Cheryl Benton for her continued support.

Renée for always being there.

And for all the many lost friends along the way: I am becoming until the time when I will see you all again.

ABOUT THE AUTHOR

Photo credit: Frederick Piccarello.

Marjorie J. Levine is still greatly nostalgic and believes life's journey can be as beautiful as a memoir unfolding in an old silent movie. She retired after a long career as an elementary school teacher. She is now a stand-up comic, an actor, a blogger, an internet broadcaster, eclectic artist and wistful poet. She lives alone in New York City